AF255481

Artistic Expressions of Transgender Youth

Volume 2

By Tony Ferraiolo, CPC

Publish Your Purpose Press
141 Weston Street, #155
Hartford, CT, 06141

The opinions expressed by the Author are not necessarily those held by Publish Your Purpose Press.

Ordering Information: Quantity sales and special discounts are available on quantity purchases by corporations, associations, and others. For details, contact the publisher at orders@publishyourpurposepress.com.

Edited by Karen Eng
Page layout by Maura Gianakos
Printed in the United States of America.
ISBN# 978-1-946384-91-1
Library of Congress Catalog Card Number 2015914718
Second Edition, October 2019

What people are saying…

Deborah Eve Grayson, PhD, LMHC Clinical Sexologist, Licensed Mental Health Counselor

Existential questions often assist in leading us to a healing path where we can consider dynamic options that may not have been apparent otherwise. In Tony Ferraiolo's Artistic Expressions of Transgender Youth *series, he poses formidable questions and how they are interpreted by transgender youth are startlingly authentic, raw, and rich. Stories of struggle as well as celebration are contained within these pages filled with insight, creativity, and wisdom.*

A.C. Demidont, DO Chief Medical Officer, Anchor Health Initiative

The Artistic Expressions of Transgender Youth *series is an invaluable tool for any office that works with Trans* and Gender Expansive Youth! A picture is truly worth a thousand of my words when our office attempts to educate families and other medical providers on the thoughts and emotions that Trans and Gender-Nonconforming (TGNC) youth experience on a regular basis. I would highly recommend this book be part of the toolbox used by medical and mental health providers as part of working with TGNC youth and the families who love them.*

Mimi Lemay Advocate and Author

Tony Ferraiolo's Artistic Expressions of Transgender Youth, Volume 2 *is a powerful addition to the toolbox of any therapist, advocate, educator, or parent who wishes to have greater insight into the experiences of actual transgender youth. The artistic renderings of youth struggling with the unique challenges—and triumphs—of gender non-conforming identities, contain a roadmap toward ways we can help these children thrive.*

Michele M. Mom of an Awesome Son

As a mom of a transgender son, the Artistic Expressions of Transgender Youth *book series helped me understand the struggles that my child was experiencing. Before I read* Artistic Expressions of Transgender Youth, *as a parent I was terrified at how to lead my child's life and advocate for them. But now I know that a happy and fulfilled future is not only a possibility but a probability.*

Acknowledgments

To my family: Mom, Dad, Frank, Nick, Felix, Sue, Claudia, Jennifer, Matthew, Stephanie, and Angelina, thank you for continuing to support me through my journey.

To Dru Levasseur, thank you for giving me the confidence to live my truth every day.

To Dr. AC Demidont, Christy Olszewski, PhD, Susan Boulware, MD, Anisha Patel, DO, and Stuart Alan Weinzimer, MD, thank you all for providing a safe, respectful, and caring environment for transgender and non-binary youth to access medical care. But most of all, thank you for believing in them.

To David Tate, PhD, Vanessa Pomarico, APRN, and Kathryn Tierney, APRN, thank you all for your support and caring for me—body, mind, and spirit.

To the amazing artists in this book: Hannah, Taylor, Luca, Ross, Kristopher, Mordecai, Alex, Rain, Maeve, Kasper, Edgar, Haly, Jay, Max, Lia, Vannessa, Alyx, April, thank you for sharing your emotions. Your bravery will help so many.

This book is dedicated to all parents who are honoring, loving,
and comforting their transgender and non-binary children down the road to happiness.

Foreword

by Jazz Jennings

I remember at age four when I, too, picked up a pen and sketched my emotions into a visual form of art. The drawing I created displayed a young girl who was crying because she wasn't allowed to wear a dress to school. The tears rolling down the face of the girl expressed the true devastation she felt when being denied her authenticity. The drawings in this book remind me of the creations I made during my transition. Art was a way for me to convey my internal thoughts in a bold and passionate format. For many people, drawing is a limitless and imaginative method to express their unfiltered selves. That is why the series *Artistic Expressions of Transgender Youth* is so powerful and important. It gives a reader glimpses into the raw emotions of transgender youth who have faced endless battles in the fight to be who they are. Seeing something so personal and authentic makes a huge statement and displays the ups and downs of being a transgender individual.

Over the years Tony Ferraiolo has provided a safe space for transgender youth to express themselves, with no fear of being judged or misunderstood. And in doing so, Tony has given us the perfect book series to educate parents, educators, and medical and mental health providers in a unique way—through the drawings and words of such brave kids.

Artistic Expressions of Transgender Youth provides depictions that not only relate to trans people, but to anyone who has ever experienced adversity.

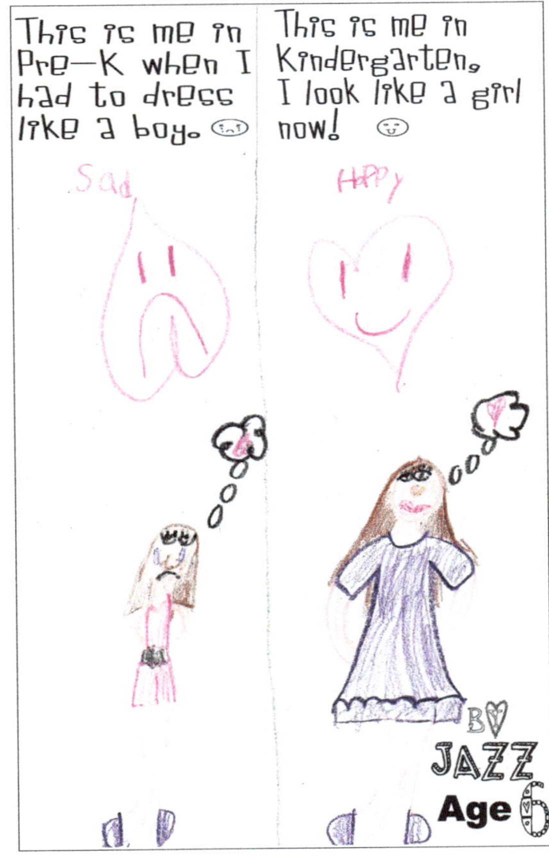

"Little Girl Crying because she's not allowed to wear a dress to pre-school" by Jazz, age 6

Preface

I am so excited to be able to bring to you *Artistic Expressions of Transgender Youth, Volume 2*. After hearing from so many parents, educators, and medical and mental health providers about how much the first volume helped them realize how their presence in a transgender or non-binary child's life can either help them live a happy, healthy, and productive life or lead them down a path of depression, self-harm, or even suicidal ideations, I knew that a second volume with two different questions would help them even more.

When I train educators and health and mental health providers, I use artistic expressions as one of my workshops. As I go through each slide, I remind my audience that I am simply a vehicle for the voices of transgender and non-binary children. For some reason, when the audience can see the emotions they believe the pain. We need to believe the words when these children say them. This can greatly minimize their pain.

Some of the drawings bring them to tears while others cause them to gasp due to the shock of the pain that some of these children are in. I gently ask how can they not honor them? How can they not call them by their preferred name and pronoun? How can they outright deny them the use of a bathroom? Or deny them access to the medical care they so desperately need? I can tell you that after they sit through a workshop, you can feel the shift in the room. More times than I can count, I am approached afterward by audience members who say, "OMG I didn't know, I didn't realize that what I was doing was causing such pain." My answer to them is pretty much the same every time, "Well, now that you know, I'm sure you will change the way you are communicating with them."

As I received the feedback from so many, I remember saying to myself, "Wow, the book hit my target audience." I was ecstatic!

But then I heard about another group of people who were purchasing the book, transgender and non-binary youth. Most of them lived in areas in our country where little or no support is offered—places where they feel so alone and hopeless, places where they could never be their authentic selves. A few of these children have reached out to me and have told me how the book has helped them, mainly because they don't feel alone. One child said, "At least now I know I'm not a freak or that I wasn't born wrong." It is so heartbreaking to think that so many children are out there suffering and living in such pain. But knowing that *Artistic Expressions of Transgender Youth* is helping them survive provides me with one more good reason to put together Volume 2.

I am hoping this book reaches the people who need it the most. That after they read this volume, they will change the way they view transgender and non-binary youth, that it will bring them to a place of understanding how the struggles are real and the dreams are heartfelt. You see, I don't expect anyone who doesn't identify as transgender to understand what it is like to be transgender. And if you are doing that, well you are setting yourself up for failure. I could never understand what it feels like not to be transgender, but I still respect those who are not transgender. To me it is all about kindness, compassion, and understanding that everyone deserves to be happy.

Every one of our journeys has a beginning and an end, but it is what you do in between that truly matters. We are the only ones who can make it either an amazing, happy journey or a journey of struggle. A lot of times transgender and non-binary children's journeys begin with confusion and fear. We must make this part of their journey as short as possible. Or better yet, accept them for who they are and eliminate the confusion and fear altogether.

What makes you sad?

During my ten years of working with transgender children, I learned early on that seeing their sadness and feelings of hopelessness would be the hardest part of my work. But I also realized that if I didn't ask them what made them sad, I could never help them to the path of happiness.

As I explained in *Artistic Expressions of Transgender Youth Volume 1*, the first question I ever asked the children to draw their emotions around was, "What makes you sad?" This was all because a very brave six-year-old shared her emotions that day. When asked why she felt sad, her answer was, "I always feel sad when I can't be who I know I am." The only reason she answered me was because the art group was a safe space, a place where she knew she wouldn't be judged or bullied. A place where everyone was honored and loved for who they are, not for who everyone else wanted them to be.

It really hit home for me the first time a mom asked me to visit her thirteen-year-old trans son who just attempted suicide and was admitted to a psych ward. I remember when the mom called, her voice was shaky and filled with panic, "Tony…my son is in the hospital, do you go to hospitals to see kids?" I was instantly heartbroken and very quickly answered yes and made plans to go for a visit. He didn't know I was coming. This was new ground for me; the only time I was ever on a psych ward was when I was a patient, so I took a deep breath and was buzzed into the ward.

I remember looking around, seeing children who were clearly medicated, a few crying, and one crying out for their mommy. The nurse put me in a room and within in a few minutes, he walked in the room. When he saw me, a big smile came over his face, and he screamed, "Oh my God! Tony! It's you!!" My heart melted. The smile didn't last too long as we began to discuss what led him to be hospitalized. What do you say to a thirteen-year-old or any child when they say, "I just don't want to live anymore."? How do you empower them to own their truth and help them walk their own path, when almost everyone in their lives is blocking them from doing so?

As you will see in this chapter, most of their sadness and distress comes from external influences not internal influences. When their parents or health and mental health providers tell these children that they can't be who they know they are, or when schools do not educate themselves on their transgender students and do not intervene when bullying is taking place, it can be a death sentence!

Sadness is an emotion that fuels anger. Quite often we shift away from the authentic emotion of sadness and shift to the emotion of anger to protect ourselves. This is true for adults and children. We need to stop thinking that children's emotions are not valid. We need to acknowledge the sadness, and ask how you can help them through it. So, parents, please listen, love, and hug your child. As an amazing mom once told me, when you hug your child, hug them until **they** let go.

Artistic Expressions of Transgender Youth

I asked over 100 kids to answer the following questions:

- What makes you sad?

- What do you want to be when you grow up?

This book contains 24 of the most moving responses.

What makes you sad?

Hannah

Age 6

Hiding myself...it sucks the life out of me.

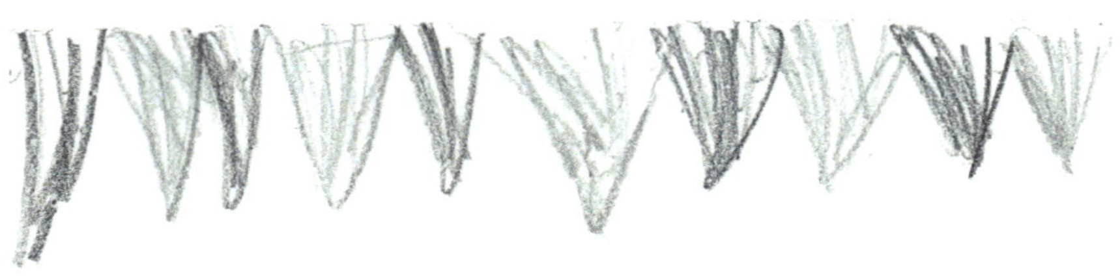

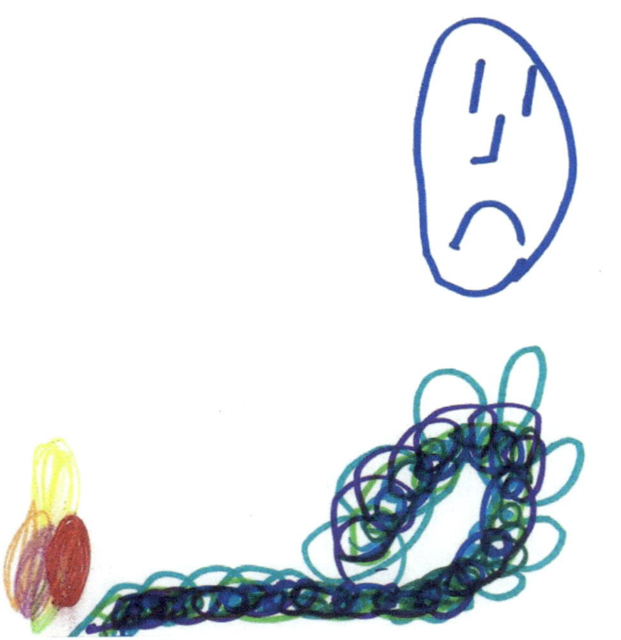

Taylor

Age 13

What makes me sad is when people don't know your situation but judge you anyway.

This picture is of shining light on those who don't understand that it's ok to be different. The sunlight represents the information that we are providing for them so they can try to understand.

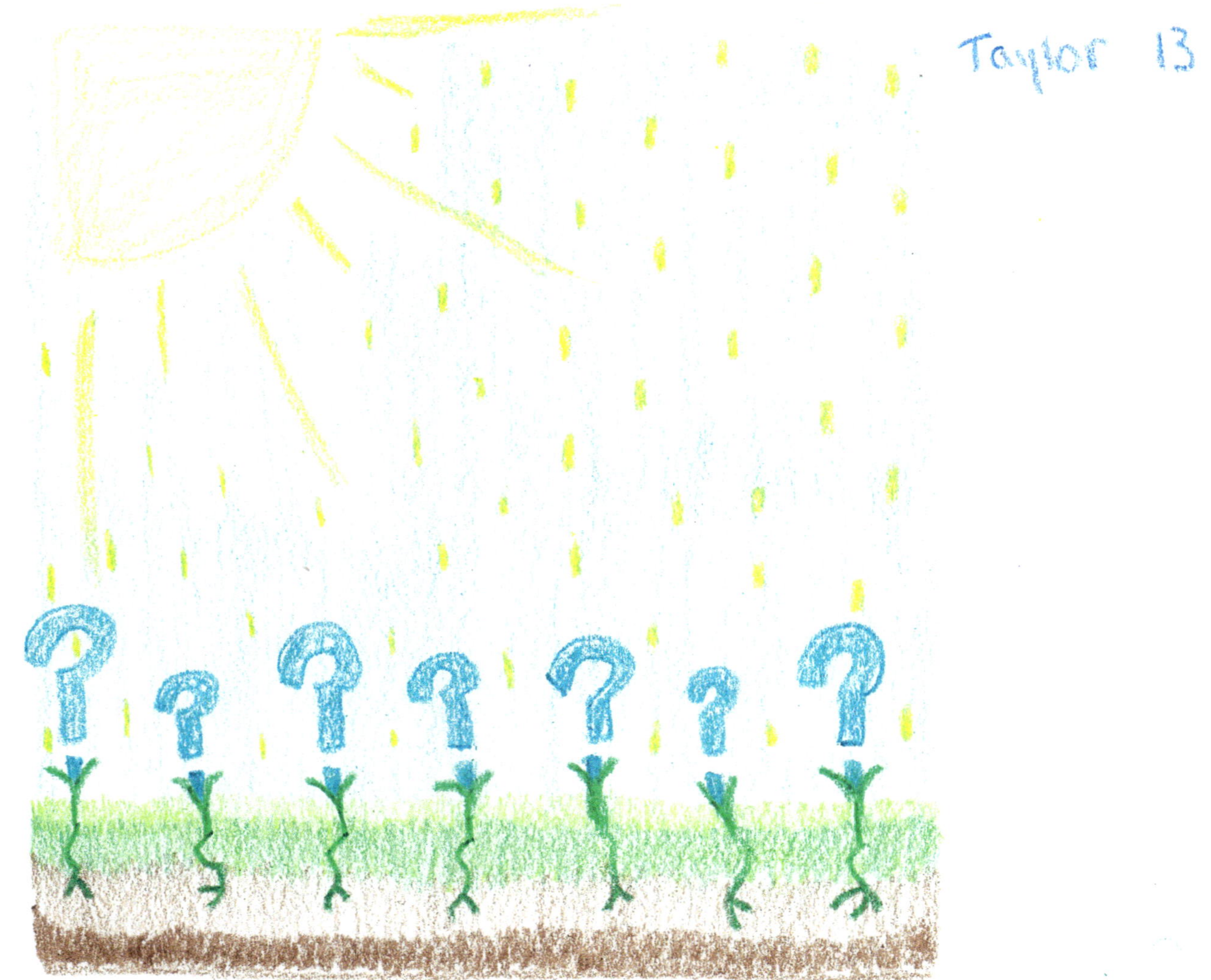
Taylor 13

Luca

Age 14

Being misgendered makes me sad.

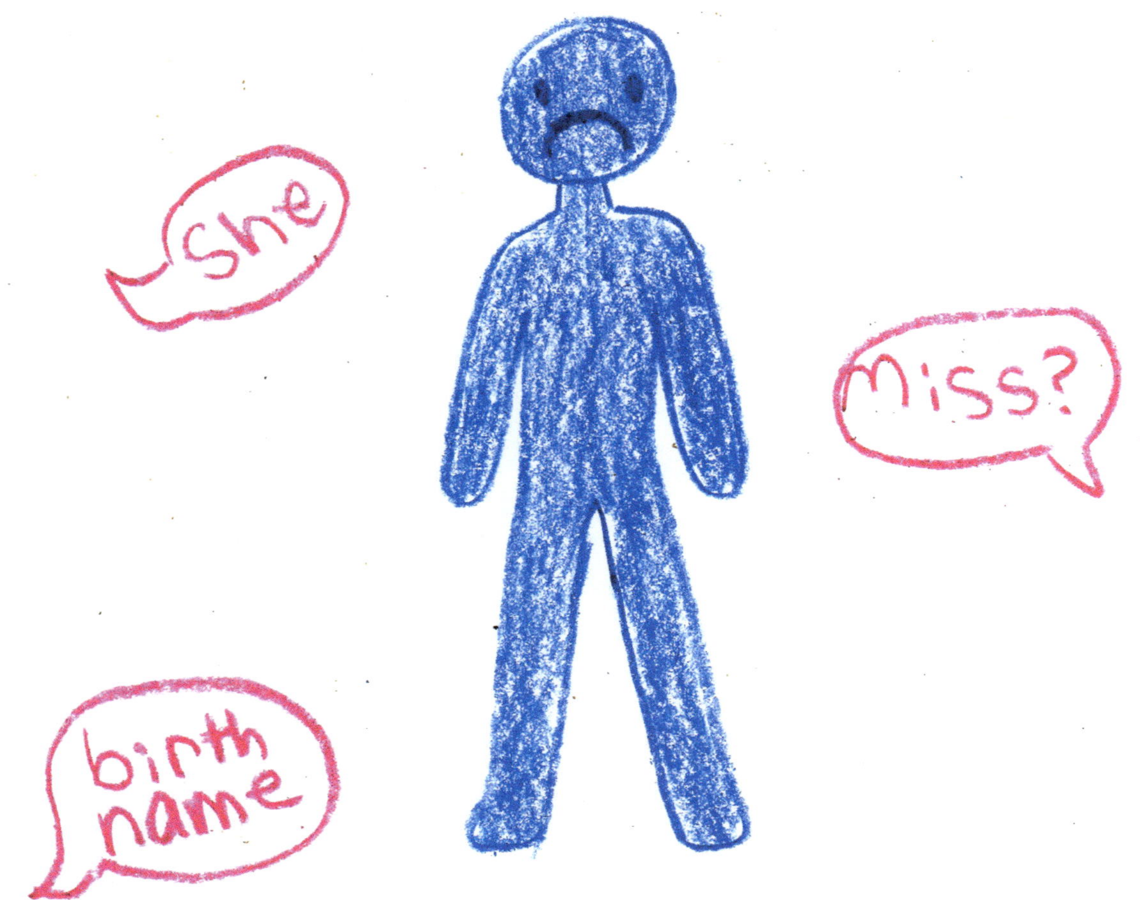
She
Miss?
birth
name

Ross

Age 14

I hate being left out because of who I am. I hate being told it is my fault for being called she. I hate being told I look too feminine to be a guy. I also hate people talking behind my back.

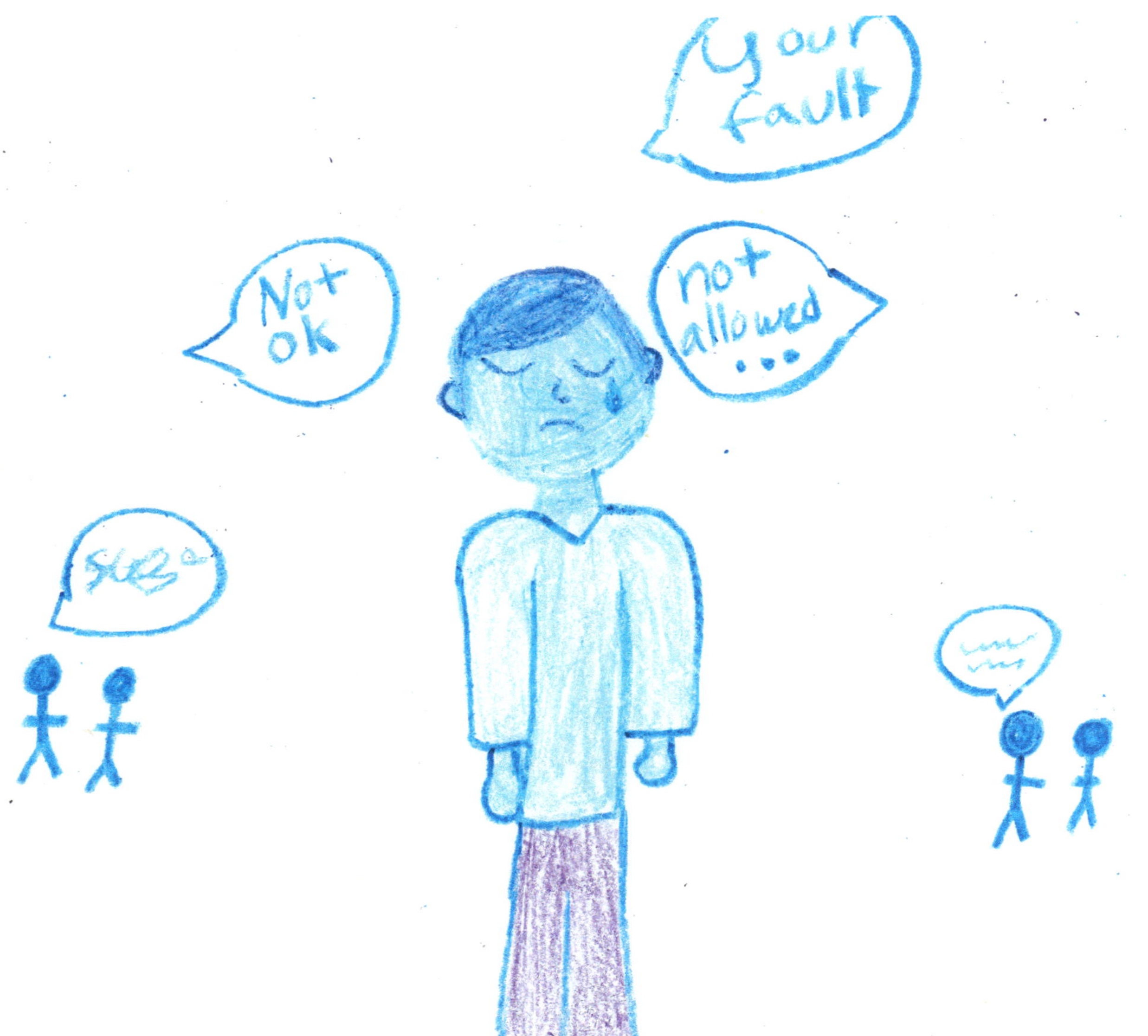

Your fault
not allowed ...
Not ok

Kristopher

Age 16

My body when I look in the mirror, the only thing that comes is sadness.

Things That Make Me Sad :
(parts of my body)
Kristopher, 16

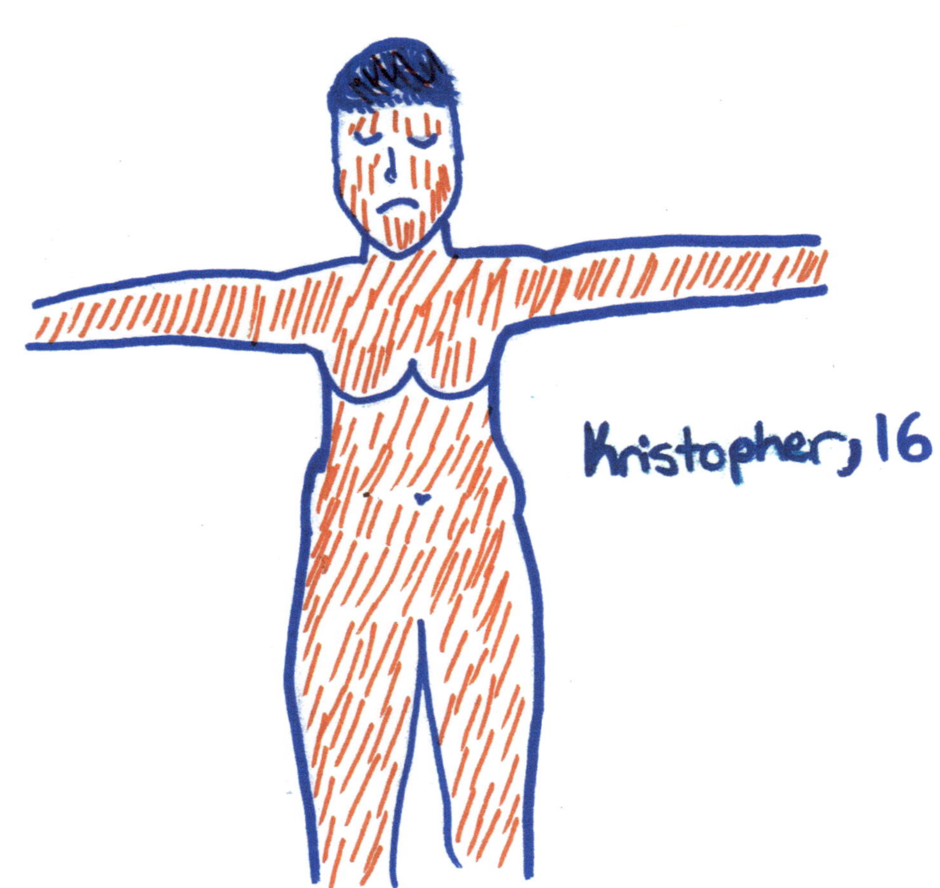

Mordecai

Age 16

When my peers do not use my correct pronouns, it makes me feel feminine. I don't know what it is about my body that still screams "girl" but it makes me sad.

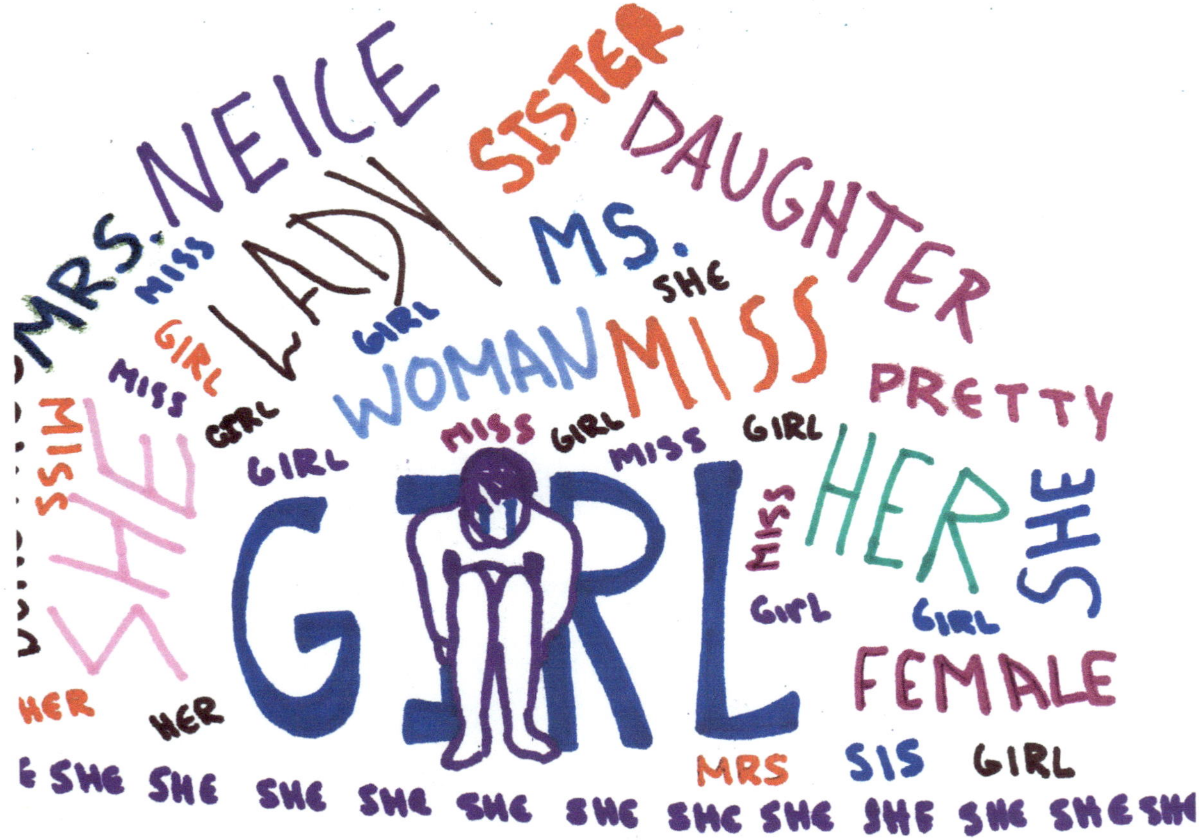

MRS. NEICE SISTER DAUGHTER
LADY MISS MS.
GIRL SHE
GIRL GIRL WOMAN MISS PRETTY
MISS GIRL
MISS GIRL MISS GIRL
GIRL MISS GIRL
SHE GIRL HER SHE
MISS
GIRL GIRL
FEMALE
HER HER MRS SIS GIRL
SHE SHE SHE SHE SHE SHE SHE SHE SHE SHE SHE SHE
MORDECAI, 16

Alex

Age 16

*When people say I **can** change things about myself,
I really wish I **could**. If only.*

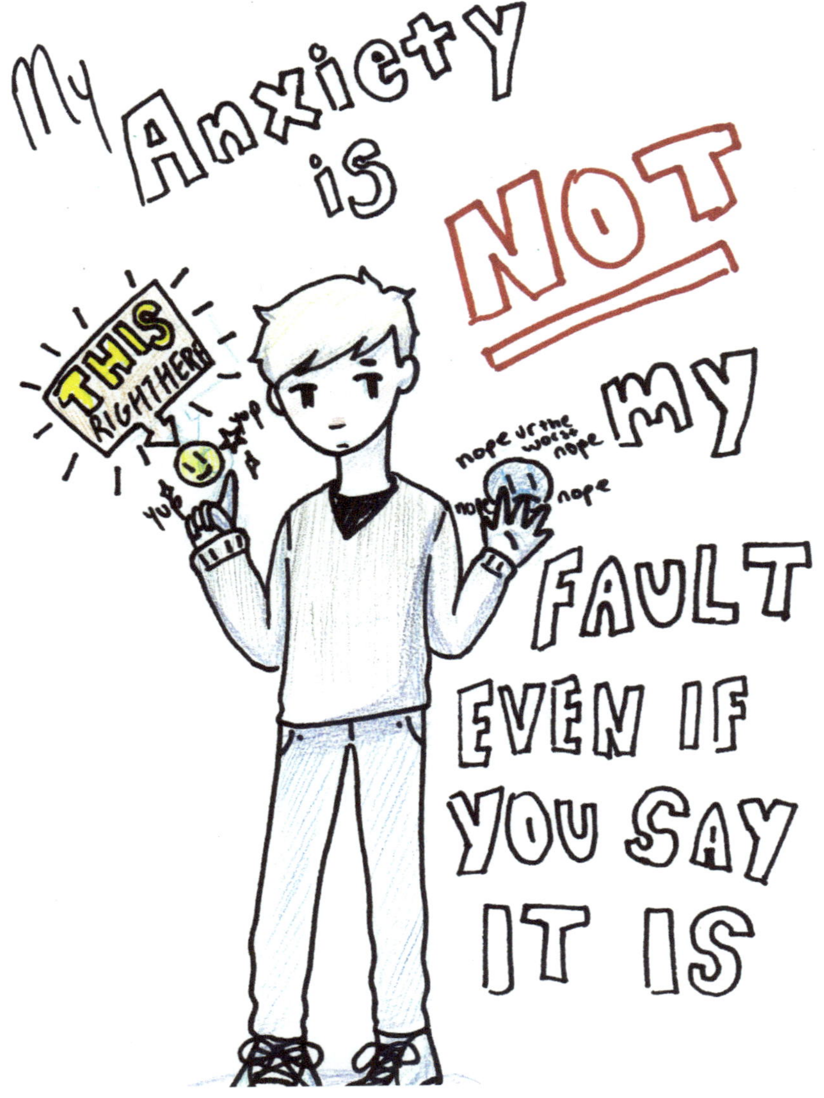
My Anxiety is NOT MY FAULT EVEN IF YOU SAY IT IS
THIS RIGHT HERE
nope
nope it the worst nope
nope
nope nope

Rain

Age 17

It makes me sad when people misinterpret each other's feelings, especially when everyone involved in the situation has good intentions but conflict arises anyway due to misunderstandings caused by the imperfections of human communications.

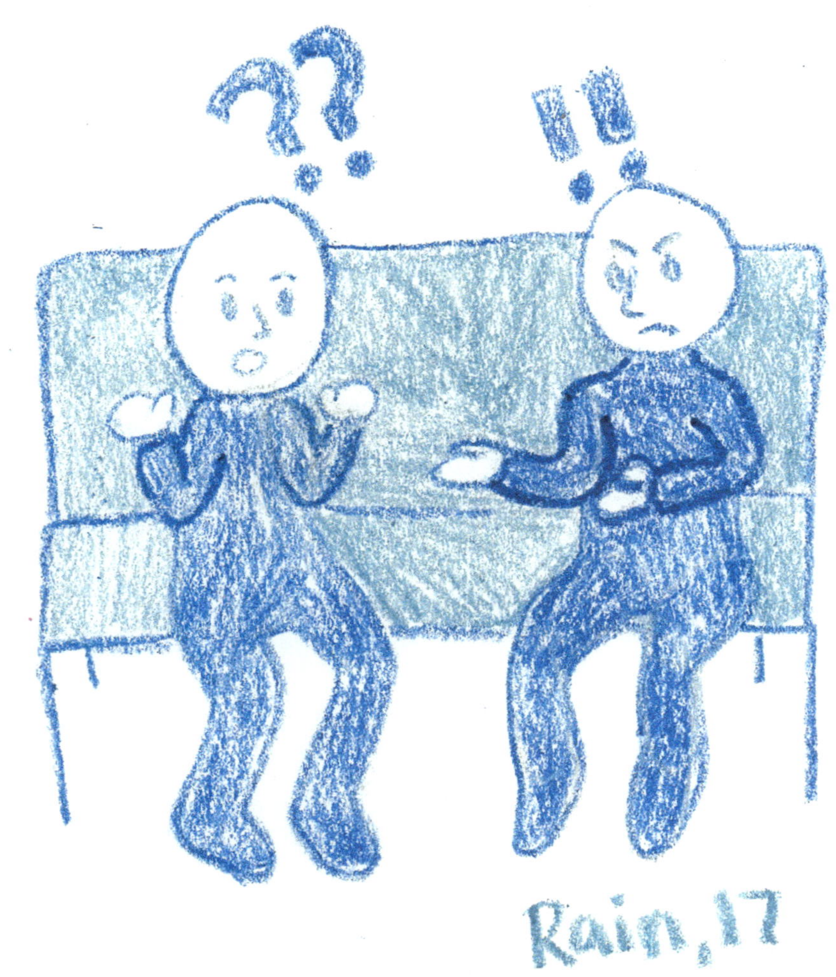

Rain, 17

Maeve

Age 17

I am sad when people label me. I become less than human, I become what people make me out to be. I am an outcast. I am ugly. I am a bitch. No one tries to look beyond these labels to see who I am.

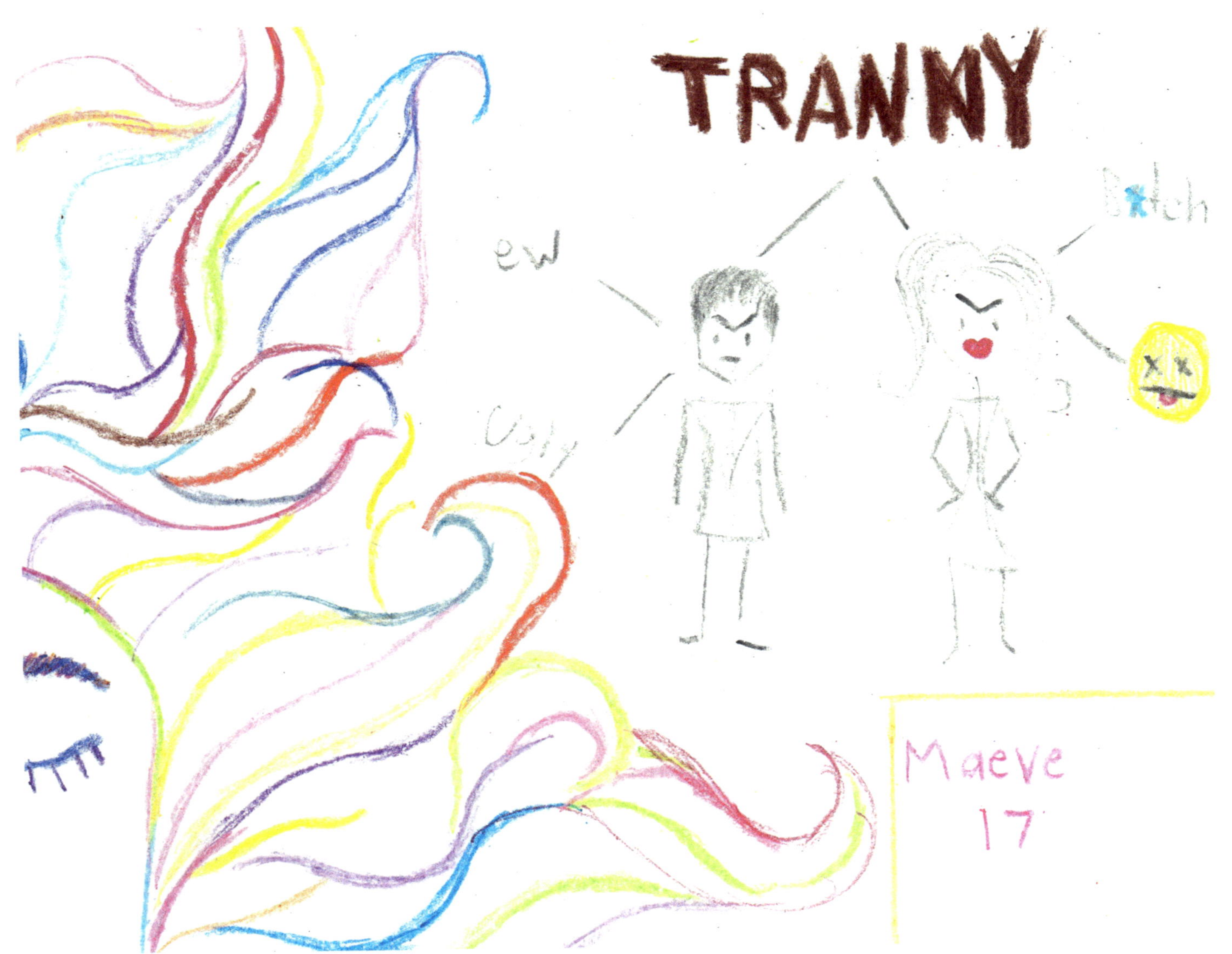

TRANNY
ew
b*tch
Maeve
17

Kasper

Age 18

I get sad when I have to get dressed and nothing seems to make me feel right. All my clothes accentuate my hips / butt / chest and it makes me miserable. I end up wearing sweatpants and a baggy hoodie & hiding in my clothes.

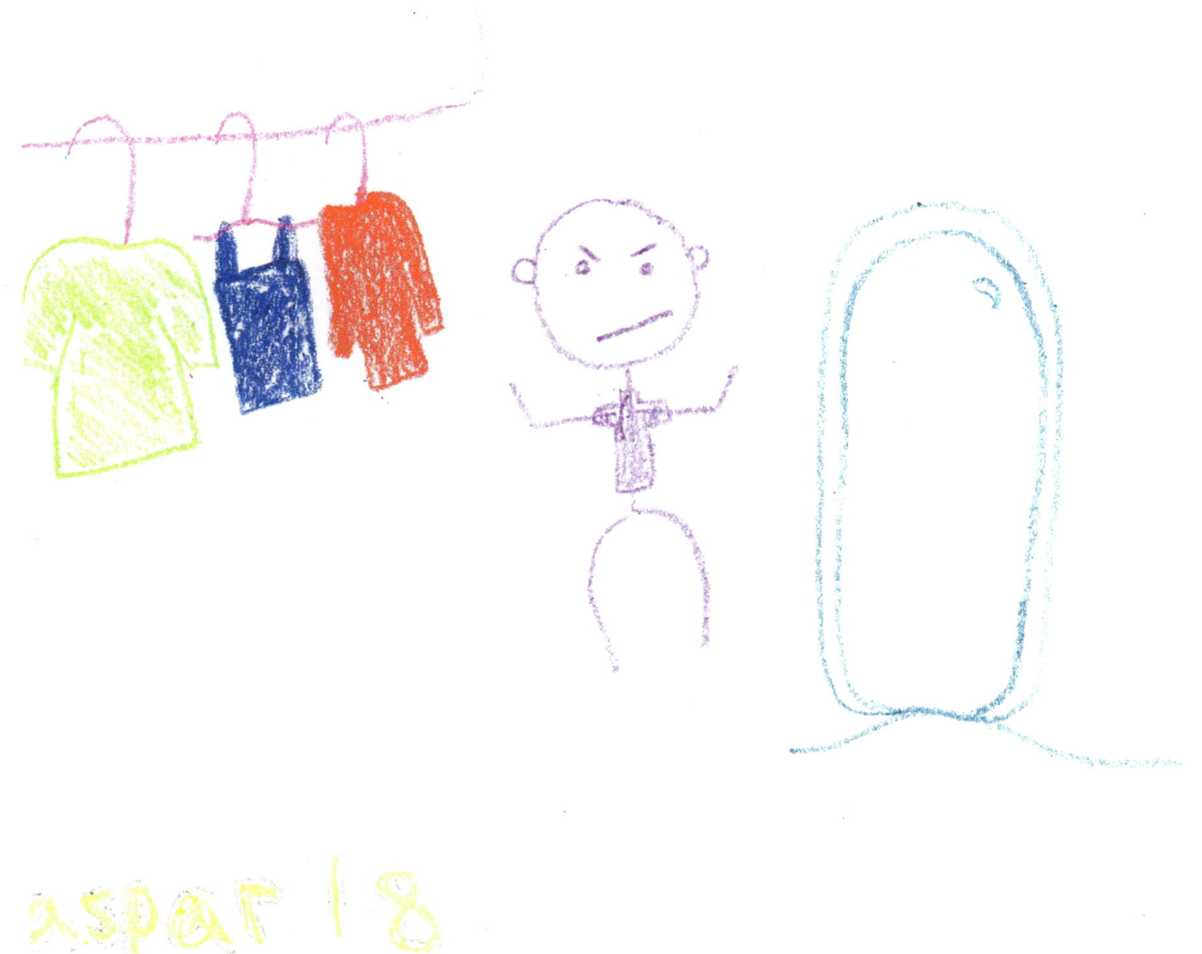

aspar 18

Name and Age Unknown

I do not want my breasts. I do not want my vagina. They do not belong with the rest of me. I do not want them. It feels as though they are separate entities working against me.

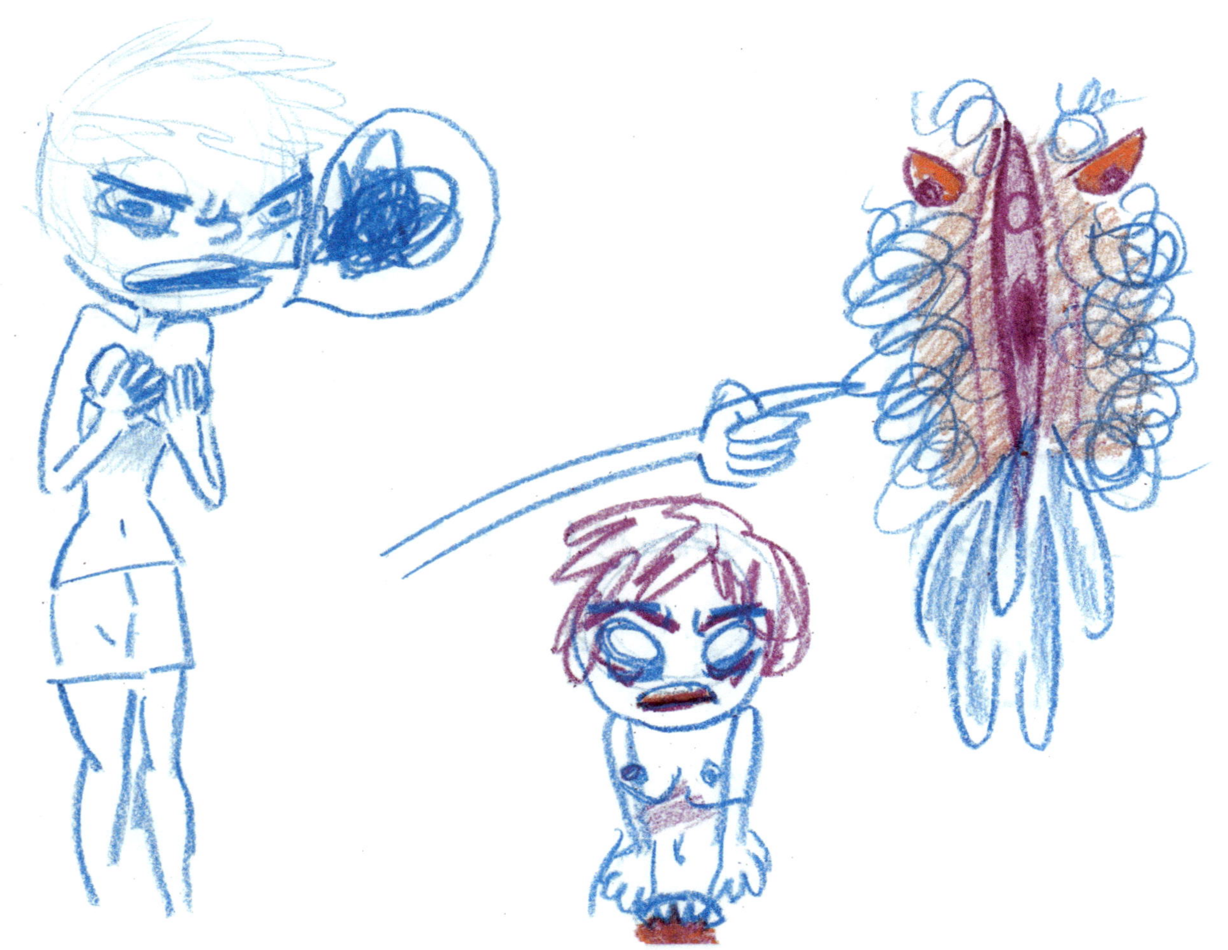

Edgar

Age 14

I drew a picture of myself holding a mask, because it makes me sad when I'm made fun of by parents and peers, and forced to present in a way that pleases people. I hate that just because society has "rules" about how people should be, that I have to fit in that mold, too.

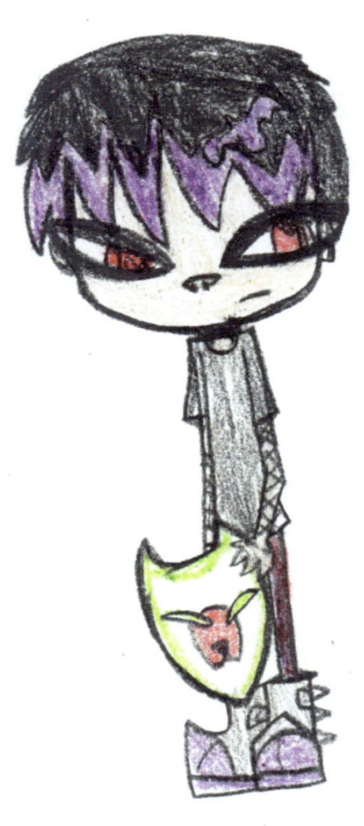

Edgar age 14

What do you want to be when you grow up?

I am sure you have asked a young child or teen this question, and some of you might remember being asked. I have asked lots of children and teens—some transgender and some not—about their thoughts on their future. I noticed a profound difference in the answer I received from some transgender children. I also noticed that the child's age made a big difference in how they answered. You will see in this chapter that the younger kids weren't focused on their gender identity at all, while some of the teens were not only focused on their gender identity, but also on their futures as moms and dads, husbands and wives.

I ask this question to the children and teens I work with in a lot of different ways. "What are your dreams for the future? You know you have the power to create yourself, so who do you think you will create?!" It is so important that we empower them to open their minds past their gender identity. We must guide them with kindness and reassure them that they will be loved, and that having a family of their own is not out of reach.

I often remind them that if I didn't stop listening to the people who were telling me that I wasn't who I knew I was and to the people who insisted that they knew me better than I knew myself, I would be an Italian woman, married with three kids and cooking pasta every Sunday! Their response is usually a smile or giggle, but then I push it a bit further and say, "No really…imagine. How happy would I be?" What I don't tell them is like many people in the trans community, I might not have made it if I wasn't able to live my truth. But I do remind them that we all share our journeys with each other. To be honest, sometimes I think about how the world would be different if I didn't have the strength to be Tony and walk my own truth. I think about all the children and families that I have helped through their struggles. It brings me to tears because I know too many transgender youth who are so misunderstood, not supported, and who may never get to be their authentic selves. Remember, we can't expect anyone to give a hundred percent of themselves if they are not allowed to be a hundred percent of who they are.

No matter what age any child is, we need to help them see that they have a future filled with love and happiness, and that the adults in their lives believe in them. We cannot hold these children and teens to our agenda. We need to allow them to explore their lives. Too often their dreams are shattered because of the fears that the people in their lives hold. They are also shattered by others who cannot believe that they can live the life that they imagine.

There are so many people who do not accept transgender youth. There are so many people who discriminate against transgender youth in schools, medical facilities, and in simple day-to-day interactions. Don't be another person who adds to their stress. Be the person who gives them hope. And like I've said so many times, if you give a child hope for a better life, they won't want to take their life. The choice is yours.

What do you want to be when you grow up?

Haly

Age 6 ½

A Runway Model and a Makeup Artist

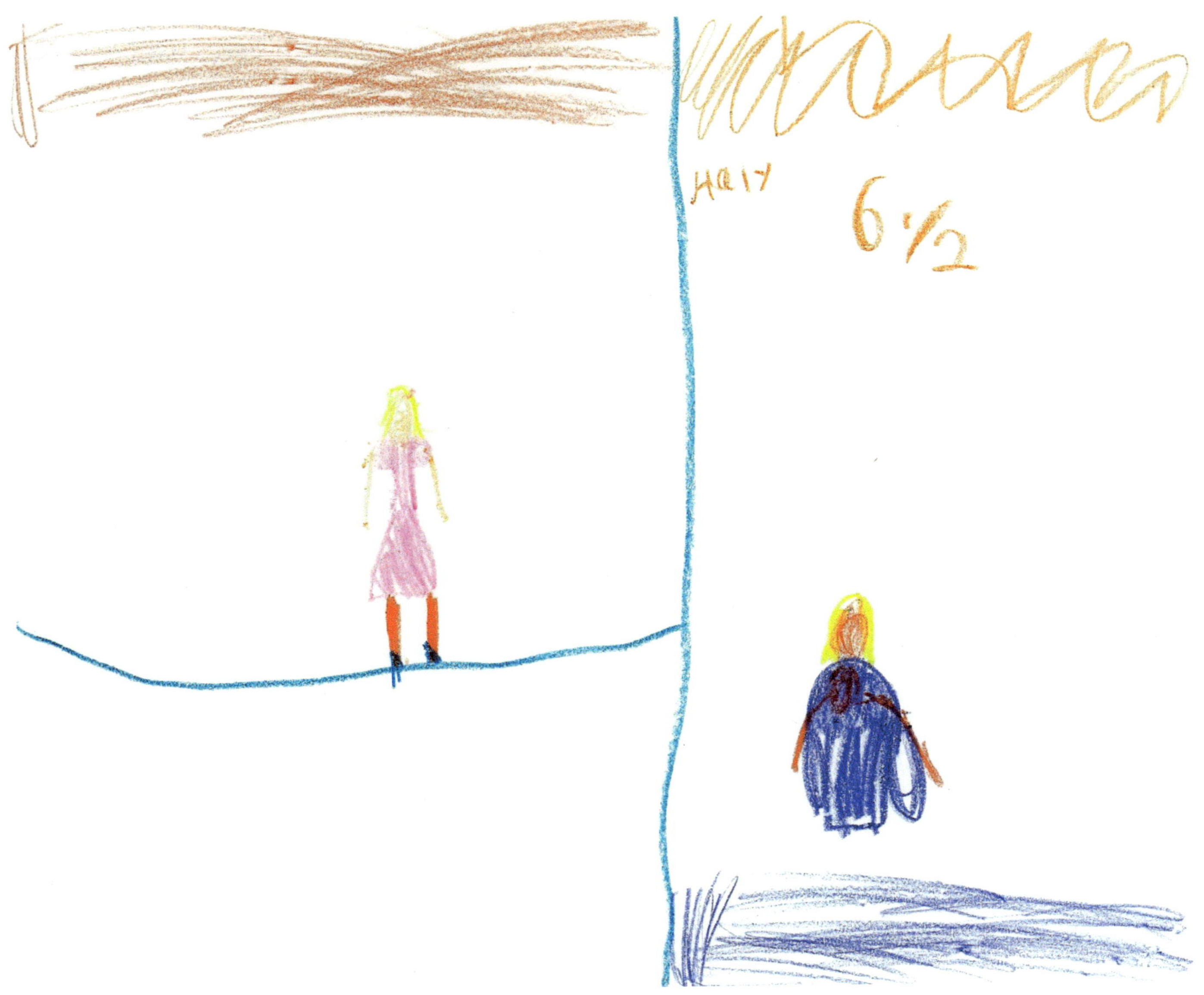
HAIY
6½

Hannah

Age 7 ¼

I want to be an Author and a Fashion Designer

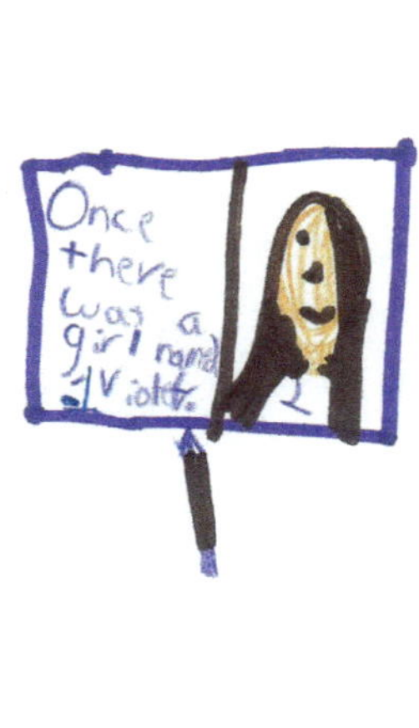

Once there was a girl named Violet.

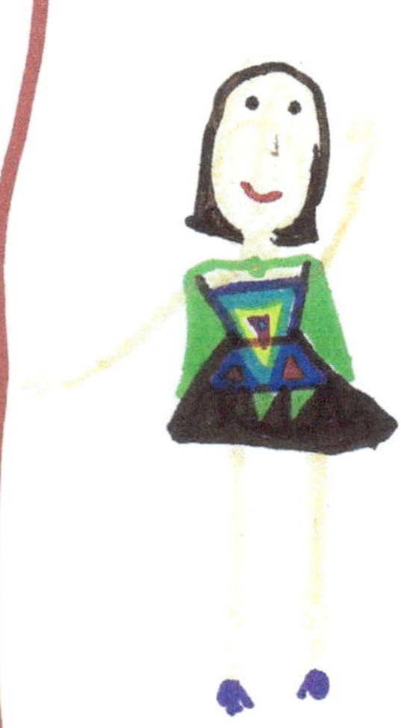

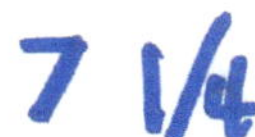

Jay

Age 8

When I grow up I want to be a babysitter of small animals and babies.

Jay   8

Taylor

Age 13

When I grow up I want to inform people about the community. Also, I want to help in the medical field so people can get hormones and surgeries that they need.

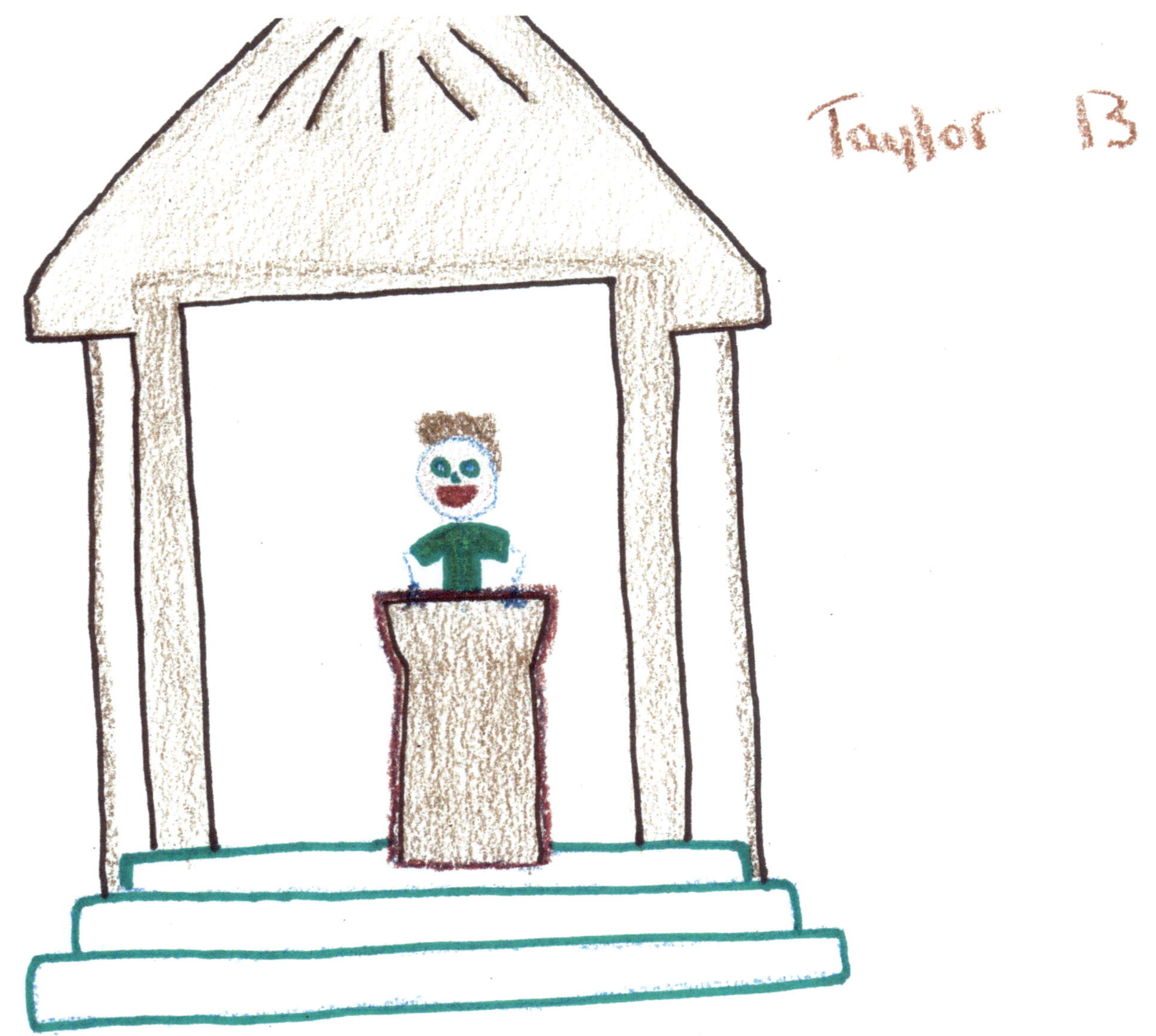
Taylor B

Ross

Age 14

When I grow up I want to be in a family.
I want to be a husband and a father.

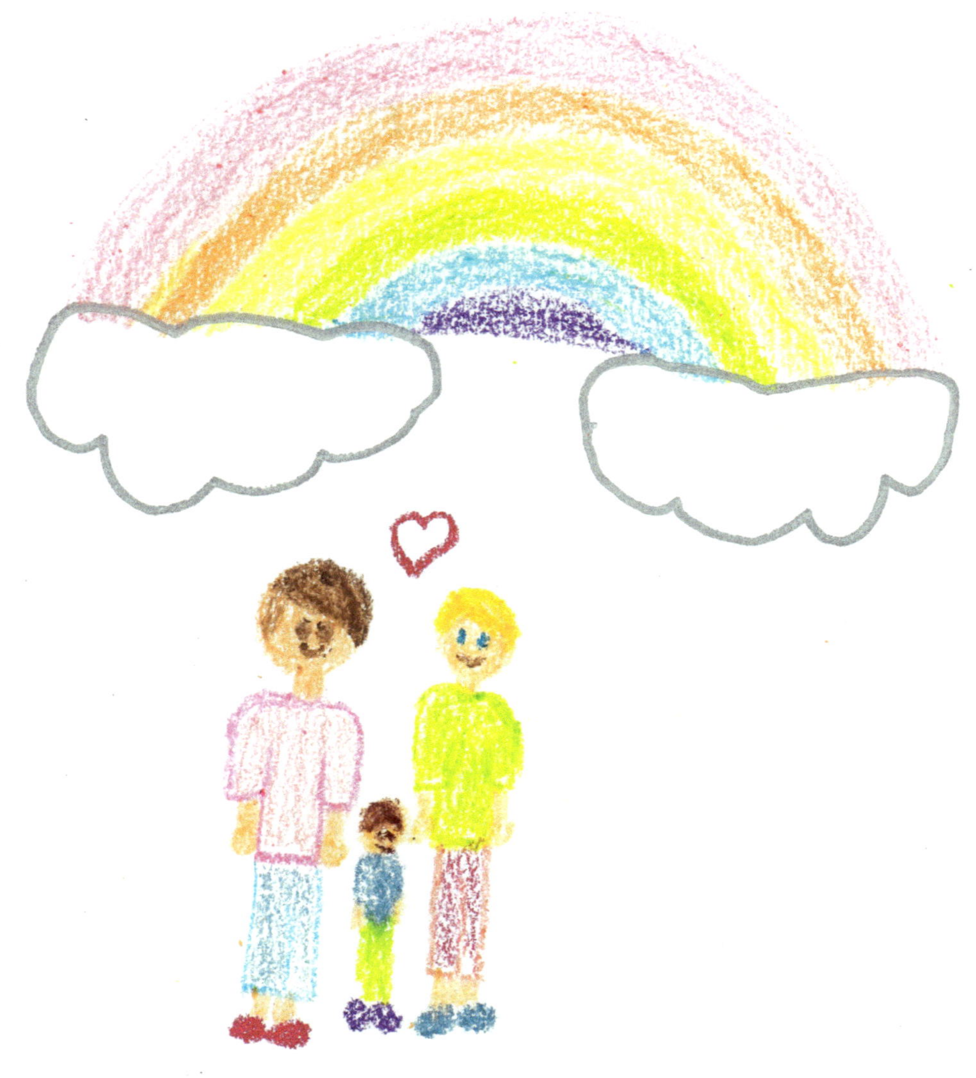

Luca

Age 14

When I grow up I want to be happy.

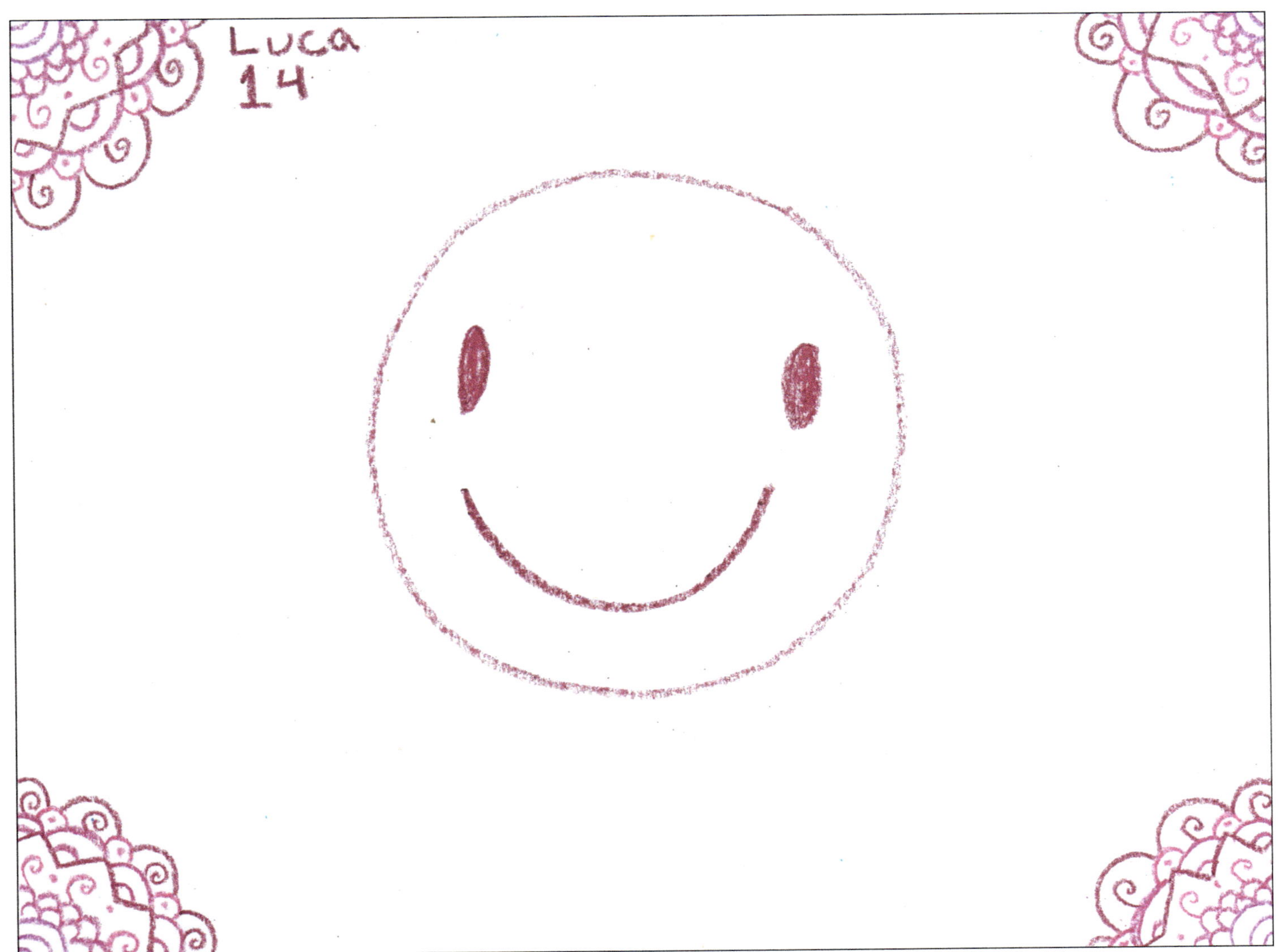
Luca
14

Max

Age 14

I want to be an author...in the next 5 years

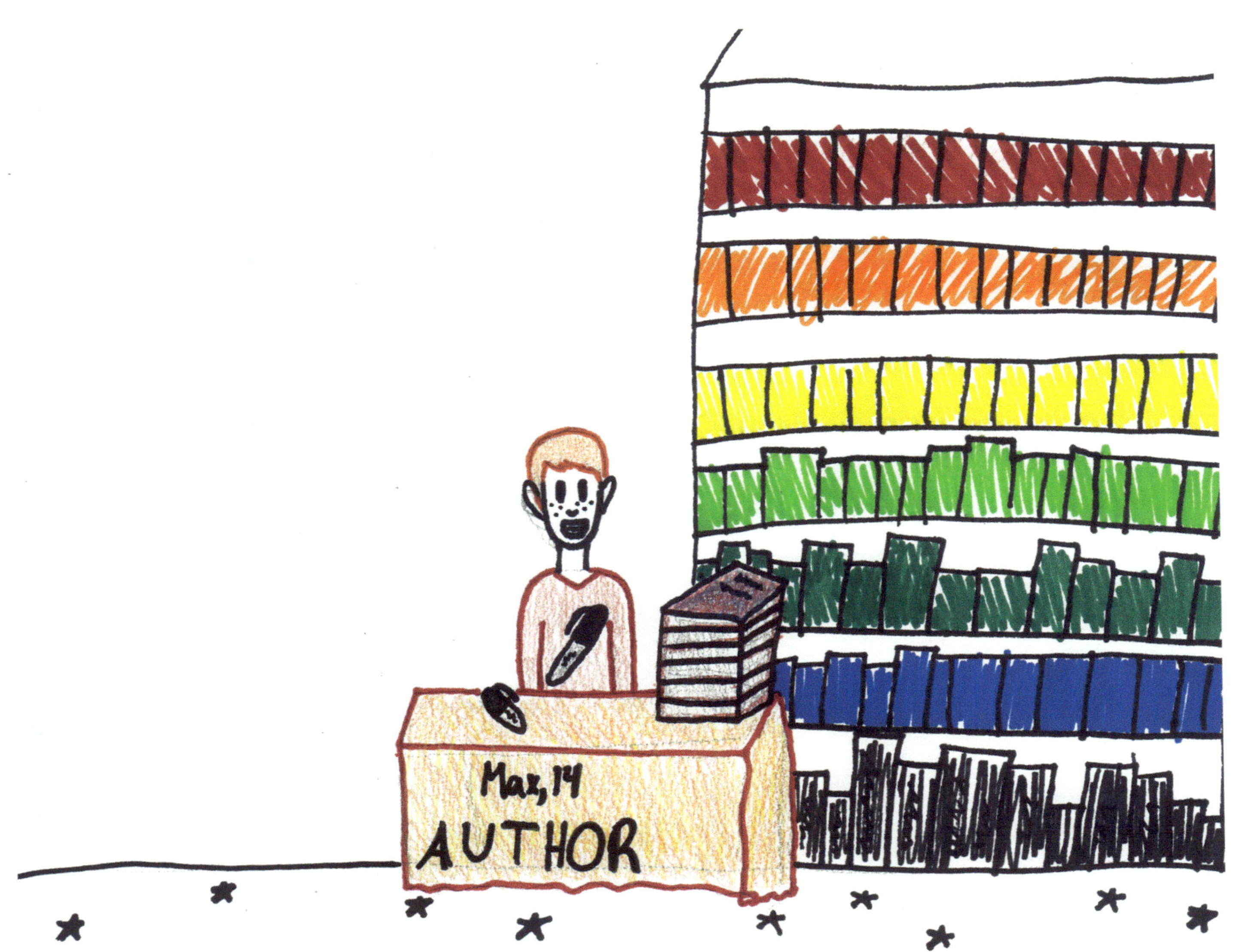

Max, 14
AUTHOR

Lia

Age 15

I want to be a Fashion Stylist.

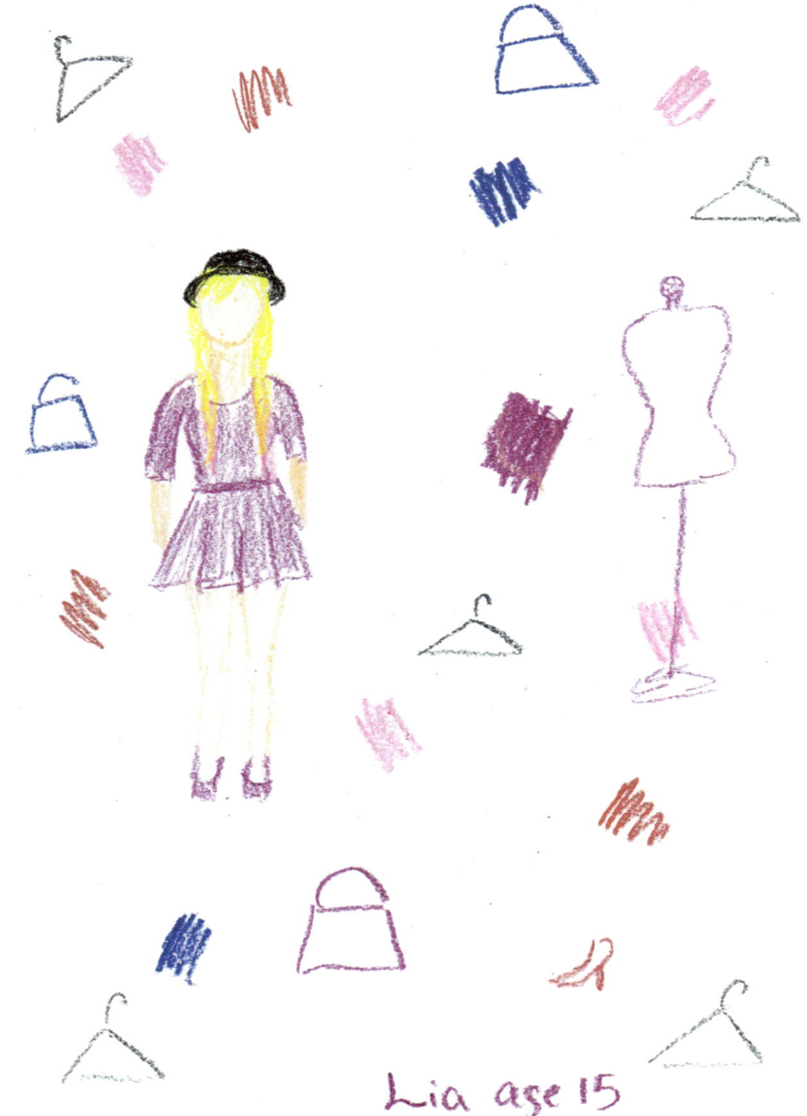

Lia age 15

Vannessa

Age 16

I wanna be a social worker to help other young kids and show them they do have RIGHTS!

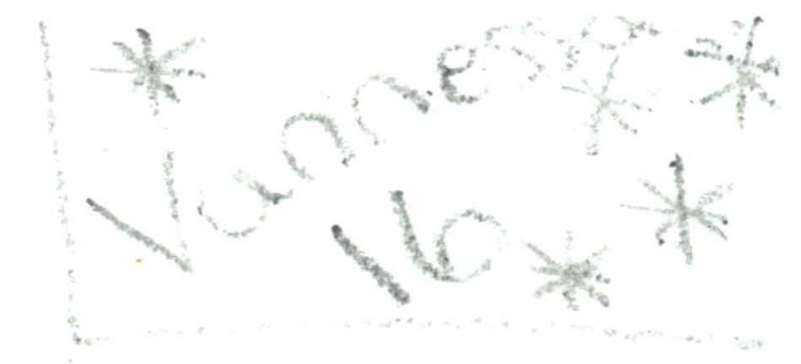

Vanessa
16

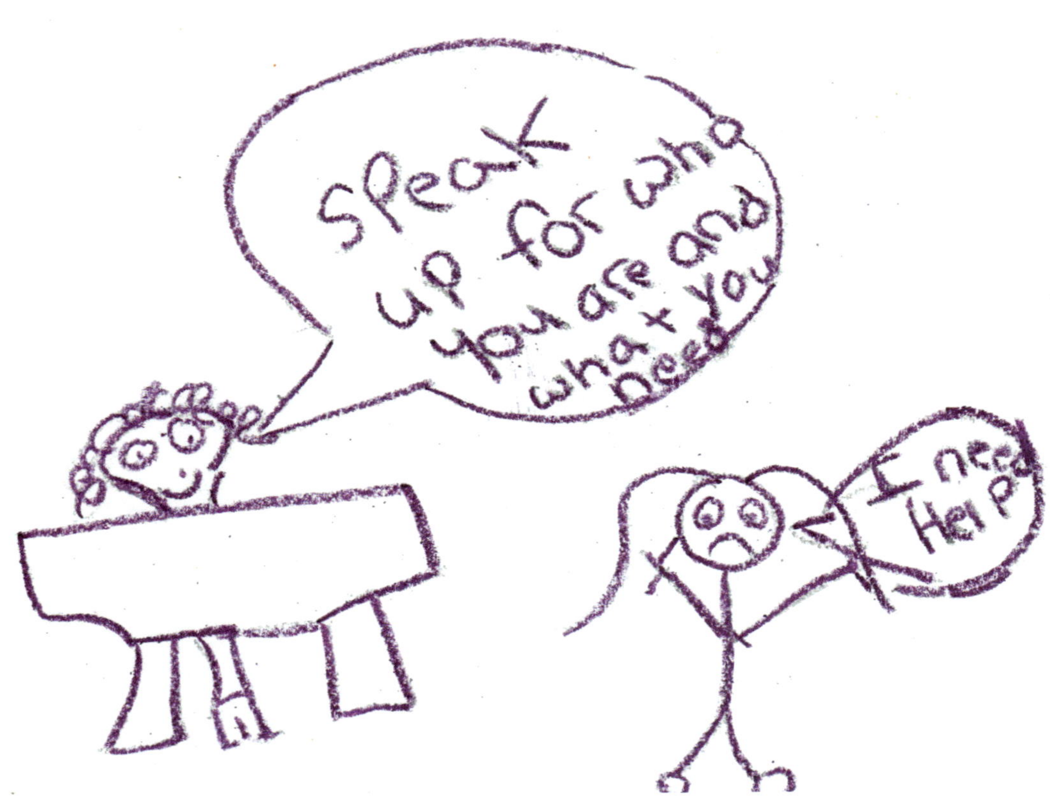

Speak up for who you are and what you need
I need Help

Alyx

Age 16

I'm not really sure what I want to do when I "grow up." But I just want to be a me that's happy.

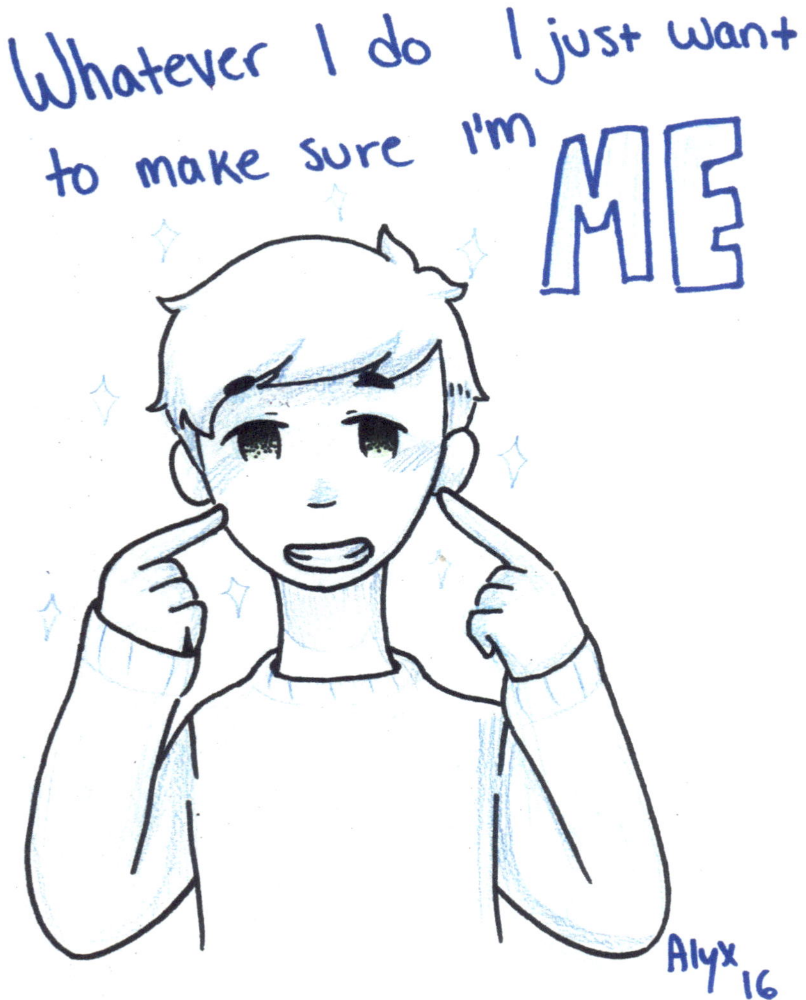

Whatever I do I just want
to make sure I'm ME
Alyx 16

April

Age 16

All the lights on me! Winning a Tony and the Oscar. Being an actress. Having the same determination I have now, wanting to be successful.

Standing up for what I believe in.

Loving what I do.

Being a role model.

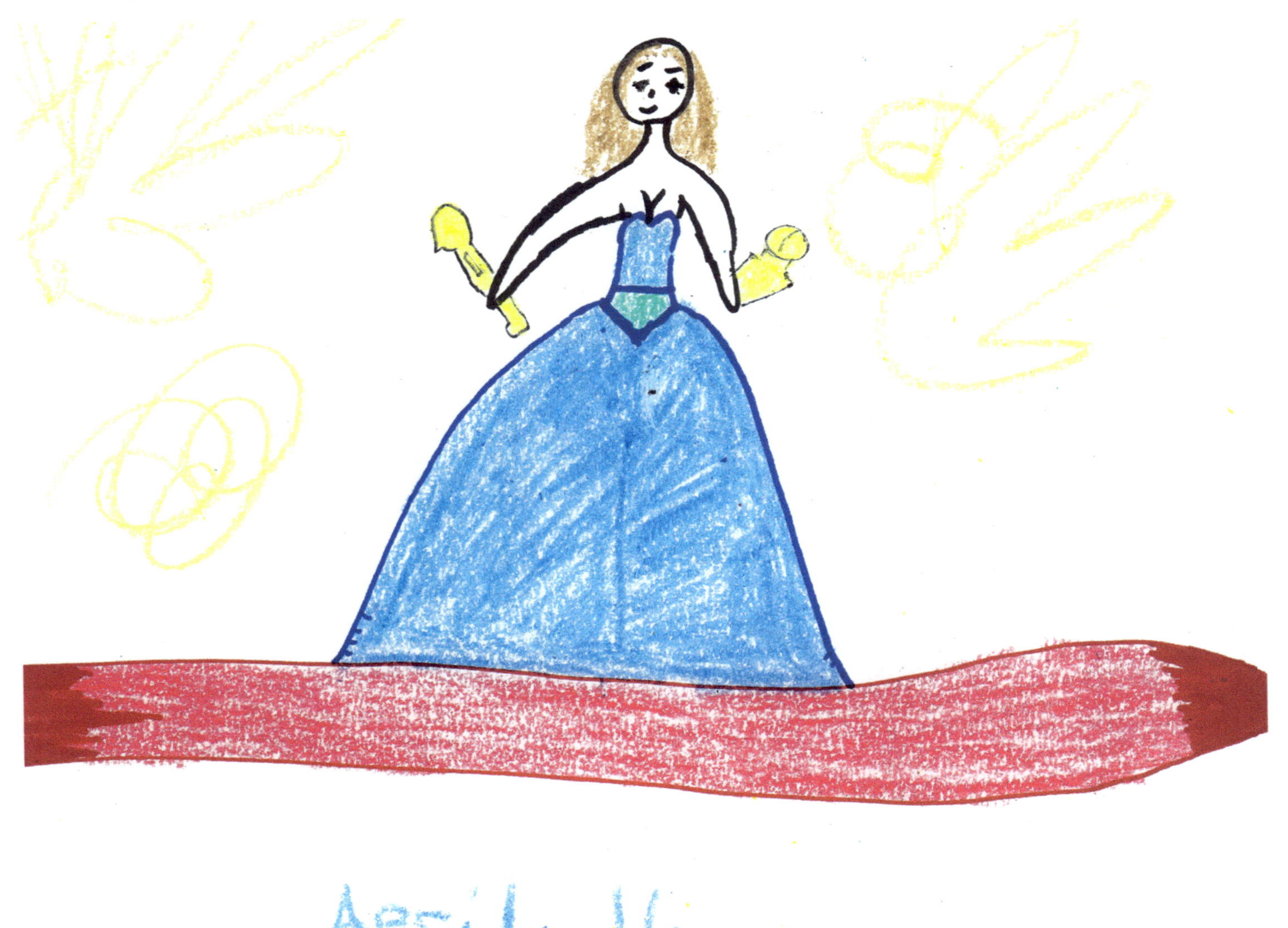

April, 16

Maeve

Age 17

I simply want to be a mother of a happy family. I won't be lonely and will be needed/ wanted and loved.

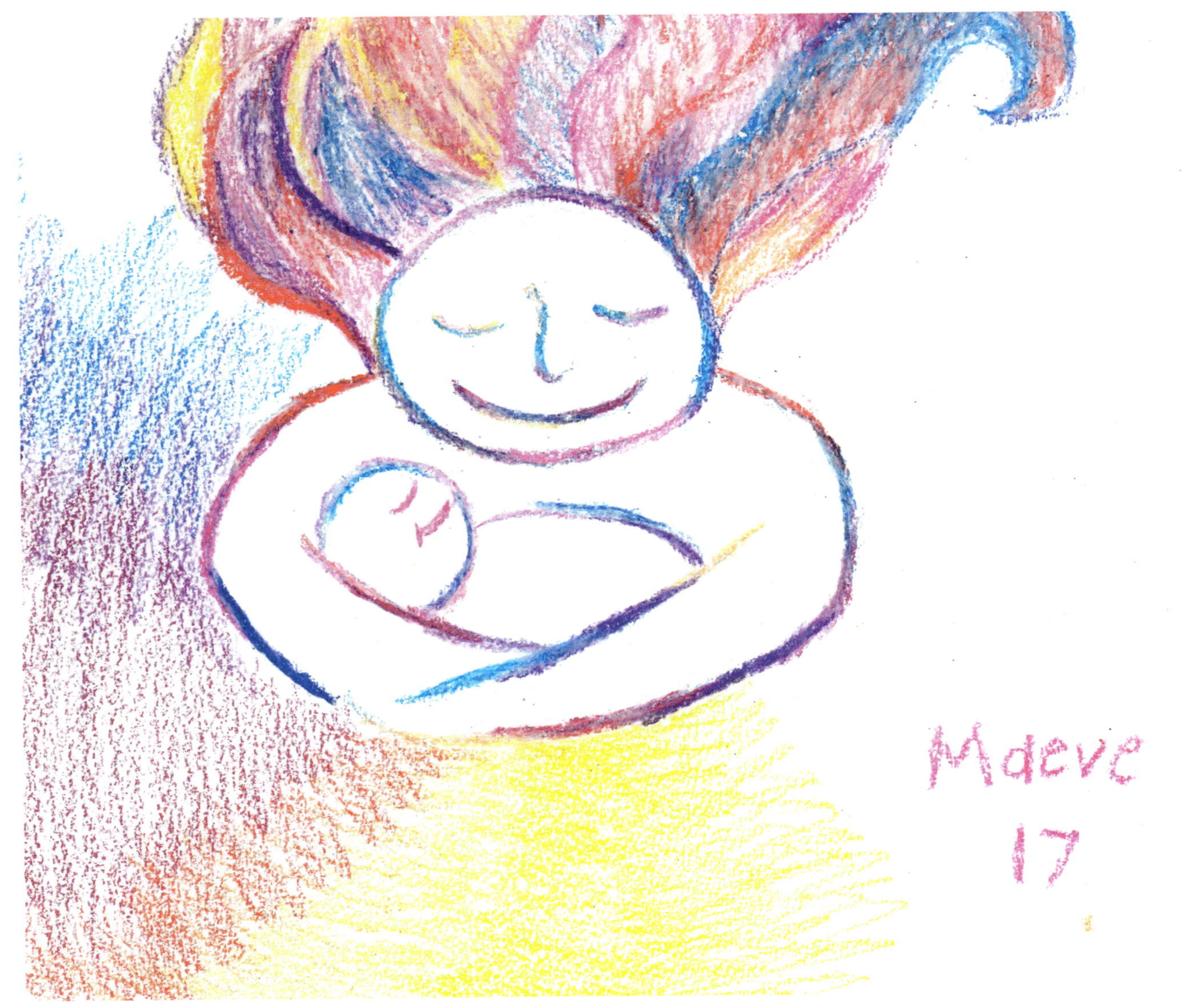

Maeve
17

A note from the author

Before I transitioned, my life had no purpose. I was the angriest person I knew, and I didn't know where the anger was coming from. I hated myself, I was not kind to others, and I didn't want to live anymore. Then my life was totally turned around after I realized that sadness was fueling all my anger. A sadness that lay deep inside my soul, it came from years of not feeling like I fit in, not feeling comfortable in my own body, and not having the knowledge of who I was: a transgender man—and that that was perfectly ok. I realized that I had the opportunity to create myself and be the person who I always wanted to be. I remember making a list, a long list of things I needed to do to create Tony. I worked hard on self-reflection, knowing that the only power I had was to change the things that I had control over changing. I remember the first thought was to be mindful of being kind.

So how did I find my life purpose? I found my life purpose in the journeys of others. I remember the moment that I realized working with transgender youth and their families was what I was born to do. Quite often I reflect on my own journey, the pain inflected to me by others and the pain that I inflected on myself. My journey, as painful as it was, created who I am today. I don't look back and think, "I wish that never happened to me." I look back and thank the universe for providing me with the knowledge to help all these children and their families down the road to happiness.

Available through Amazon

Artistic Expressions of Transgender Youth Volume 1

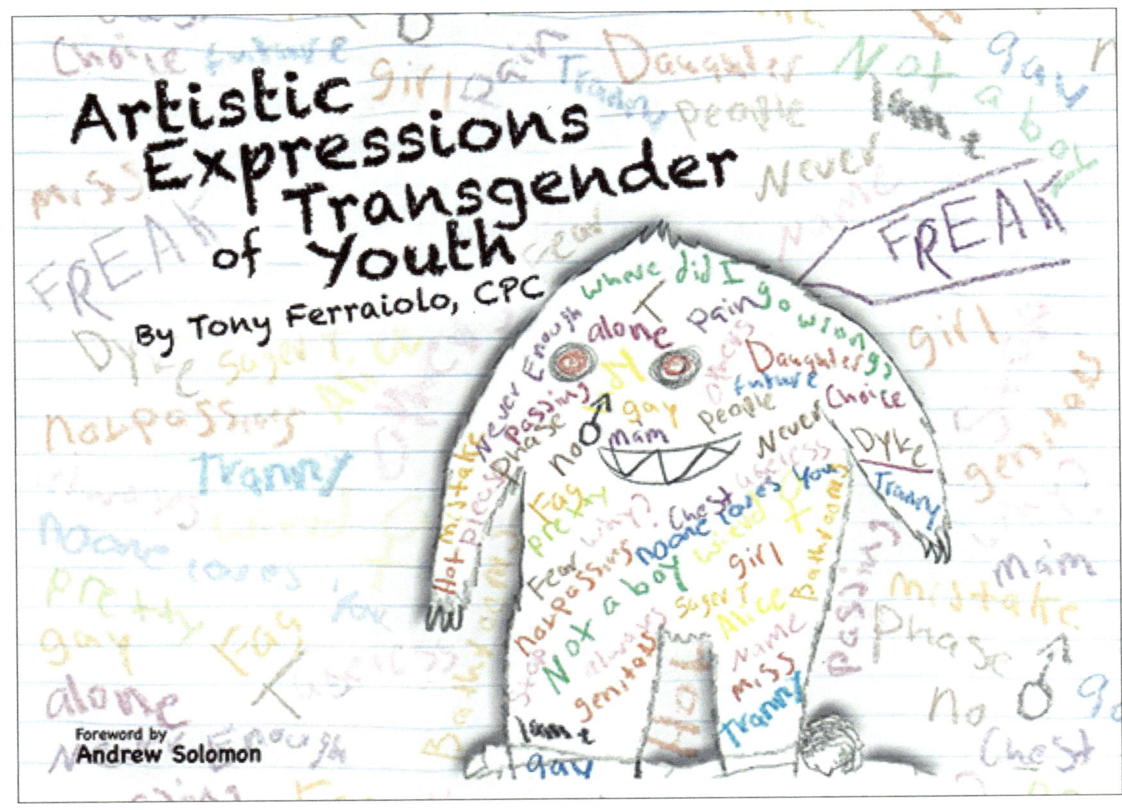

Hire Tony

Tony Ferraiolo is known as a compassionate and empowering Life Coach and as a motivating and thought-provoking trainer. Since 2005 Tony has provided trainings to over 15,000 people around the country. Tony has dedicated himself to both promoting competent and respectful health care for the transgender community, by educating providers, and advocating on behalf of patients. He also trains educators on providing a safe and respectful space for transgender children in a school environment. He encompasses a unique ability to make light of a sometimes challenging situation, putting his audience at ease so they can fully participate in his trainings, leaving them with a greater awareness of how to move forward in supporting their patients, staff, coworkers, students, and children.

If you'd like to book Tony Ferraiolo for speaking or training, please visit www.tonyferraiolo.com

See the film

Tony's life work has been featured in the award-winning documentary *A Self-Made Man* by filmmaker Lori Petchers. To book a screening please visit www.tonyferraiolo.com

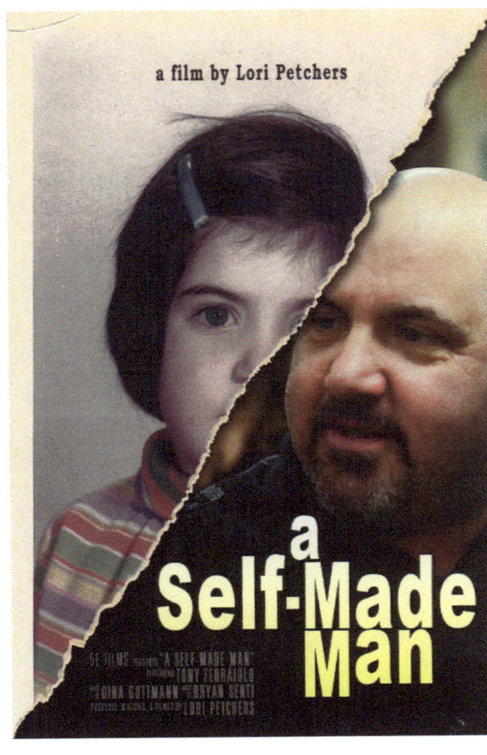

> *I will not forget who I was, I honor her. Because she had the strength to say no to the suicide, to be strong enough to survive all this and allow me to be Tony.*